BAROSSA VALLEY

KEITH P. PHILLIPS

Harvesting oats near Marananga with vineyards in background

RIGBY LIMITED • ADELAIDE • SYDNEY • MELBOURNE • BRISBANE • PERTH
First published 1972
Library of Congress Catalog Card Number 73-160564
National Library of Australia Registry
Card Number & ISBN 0 85179 337 1
Wholly designed and set up in Australia
Printed by Lee Fung Printing Co. Ltd, Hong Kong

RIGBY

BAROSSA VALLEY

"Your land will prove the kernel of this province!" the German geologist Johann Menge wrote to George Fife Angas in 1840. He referred to the land which Angas owned in the Barossa Valley; a point on which the latter needed some reassurance. His agent, Charles Flaxman, had made an unauthorised purchase of 28,000 acres at £1 an acre; a severe financial embarrassment to Angas.

Menge wrote enthusiastically about the geological prospects, including six hills of white marble; about the water resources, the fertile soil, and the charm and beauty of "New Silesia," as he called the Valley, though it had been named Barossa Valley by Colonel William Light after Barrosa ("hill of roses") in Spain.

"I am quite certain that we shall see vineyards and orchards and immense fields of corn . . . I am satisfied that New Silesia will furnish the province with such a quantity of wine that we shall drink it as cheap as in Cape Town," Menge continued prophetically. Angas helped to make the prophecy come true by inviting German settlers to take up some of the land which he now owned, and in 1842 they established the first settlement at Bethany, near Tanunda.

These German Lutherans owed a great deal to Angas. They came from Prussia and Silesia, where they had been persecuted since the 1820s for their refusal to unite their church with that of the State. One of their leaders, Pastor Augustus Kavel, went to London to seek ways in which they might migrate to a British colony, and was introduced to Angas. Angas was a wealthy merchant, deeply religious, and a director of the South Australia Company. Kavel's story struck an instant chord, and Angas advanced £8,000 to finance the Lutheran migration. The first 200 arrived at Port Adelaide in November 1838; forerunners of more than 8,000 German migrants in that era.

Many of the Germans were farmers, and they soon settled down to farming the Barossa Valley. It was subsistence farming at first; "pigs, poultry, and potatoes," but as time went by they were successful enough to repay every penny advanced to them by Angas. "The land we sow with wheat and it has provided us yearly with bread and some to sell. We have no food worries and every industrious worker, if he is not slovenly, can make ends meet comfortably," Carl Messner wrote to his German relations in 1856.

Carl Messner's list of his assets included "400 vines in bearing," and by that time a number of the Barossa settlers were cultivating patches of vines. They were following the lead set by Johann Gramp, one of the first Lutheran migrants, who took up Barossa land at Jacob's Creek in 1847. By that time the South Australian wine industry, founded by John Reynell, was almost ten years old, but Gramp was the first to produce Barossa wine. He pressed his first octave of wine, of a type which resembled the hock of his homeland, in 1850.

Gramp was soon followed by Joseph Gilbert at Pewsey Vale, Samuel Smith's Yalumba winery near Angaston, Samuel Hoffman near Tanunda, Joseph Seppelt at Seppeltsfield, the Salter family at Angaston, and other English, Australian, and German winemakers.

The wine industry grew and flourished, so that by 1972 there were over 20,000 acres of vineyards growing over the gently rolling hillsides and on the rich "flats" of the Valley. They constitute Australia's largest concentration of non-irrigated vines, and produce about a third of the nation's total output of wine through twenty-five wineries ranging from such giants as Orlando, Yalumba, and Seppelt's down to the comparatively small family establishments.

Wine is not the only Valley industry. Menge's prophecy has come true in other ways. Many farmers grow vines, but also make the Valley soils produce a rich bounty of fruit, cereal, and vegetable crops. Barossa Valley dairy farms send their milk as far as Central Australia, and the limestone from Menge's "six marble hills" is used for making cement and soda ash.

The co-operation of Briton and German which lay behind the first settlement and development of the Valley has by this time blended into an Australian community that has only the most tenuous links with the motherlands, but for a long time the German influence was very strong. The Lutherans gave to their tiny settlements such names as Gnadenfrei, Schonborn, Krondorf, Kaiser-Stuhl, Langmeil, and Hoffnungstahl. In the semi-isolation of the Valley, before motor-cars and good roads made travel a commonplace, they continued to speak a language which gradually became a mixture of German and English and was known as *Barossa Deutsch*. They retained many of their national and religious customs, such as the wearing of black bridal gowns; the "feather-stripping" before a wedding, in which a group would gather at the bride's home to make her a feather mattress; and above all the truly German love for song and music, which persists in the 110-years-old Liedertafel and the Tanunda Band Competitions.

But many of the old ways have now died out. Two wars against Germany had their effect, and the radio, cinema, and television completed the job. *Barossa Deutsch* is rarely heard now, though some Valley folk have a distinctive accent and unusual turns of speech, and the younger generation regards itself as purely Australian. The most lasting influence is that of the Lutheran religion, of which the visible and outward symbols are the thirty-six Lutheran churches. The earliest places of worship were rough and temporary, but as soon as they were able to do so the settlers built fine, solid churches with towers and spires like those in faraway Germany. Among the most imposing are those at Langmeil, Marananga (originally Gnadenfrei), Tanunda, and Dimchurch (originally Neukirch).

The character of the Barossa Valley has been formed by its size, which is only about twenty miles long by eight miles wide. It is bounded by low, steep hills, and these help to precipitate the moisture which makes the Valley look green even when surrounding areas are parched with summer. Three little rivers and numerous small creeks run out of the hills and wind through the Valley, and impelled Menge to write enthusiastically, "The Gawler . . . is flowing with more water than the Torrens had in the midst of the raining season, whilst the Torrens is as dry as last year at this time." A report written in 1849 said that, "Angas Park appears like a vast sea of foliage," and many of the huge gum trees of the Valley survive to this day. They rise, like the spires of the Lutheran and other churches, from land which has been cultivated and cherished for 130 years, and has provided a living for communities as closely settled as those of the English and European countryside. The combination of an Australian landscape with the frequent farms and townships, orchards, market gardens, vineyards, and wineries gives the Valley a character which, like that of its wines and its people, is a distinctive blend of numerous influences.

Everything seems to reflect an intense pride in home and heritage. The trimly disciplined vineyards are symbolic of the care lavished on the Valley by five successive generations, just as the orderly and imposing establishments of the older wineries demonstrate an old-fashioned pride in craftsmanship and tradition. But such things do not denote a static acceptance of the past. On the contrary, there is a vigorous acceptance of change, as shown by the modernising of many winemaking procedures and the fact that Lindsay Park, the old home of the Angas family, is now a thoroughbred racehorse stud—which produced sixty winners in one season. With its roots in the past, the Barossa Valley grows steadily into the future.

Left: These splendid gum trees near Collingrove are typical of those which adorn the roads to Eden Valley and Keyneton

This page: Two of the fine old homes of the Barossa Valley. At top is Lindsay Park, which for many years was a home of the Angas family. Now it is both office and residence for the Lindsay Park Stud. Beneath it is Collingrove, built when the Angas estate was being founded in the Valley

This page, top: Horses of the Lindsay Park Stud enjoy their own private swimming pool

This page, centre: Though winegrowing is the mainstay of the Valley, other industries are important. They include fruitdrying, as shown by these trays of apricots being laid out to dry near Nuriootpa

This page, bottom: This old stone cottage at Marananga typifies Valley architecture of the last century

Facing page, left: The descendants of German Lutherans, who migrated to the Valley in search of religious freedom, have built fine places of worship. At top is Langmeil Church, and at bottom is Tabor Church, Tanunda. In the foreground of the top photograph is the memorial to Pastor Kavel; one of those who led his flock to freedom

Facing page, right: The rich Valley soils yield bountiful cereal crops as well as grapes, vegetables, and fruit. This paddock of ripening grain is on the western slopes of the Valley

Overleaf: A true Valley scene; acres of vineyards over rolling hills. Those in the picture surround the Seppeltsfield winery

1838 1938
DEM GRUNDER DER
EVANG LUTH KIRCHE
IN AUSTRALIEN
PASTOR LUDWIG CHRISTIAN AUGUST KAVEL

Facing page: Soon after the harvest was reaped from this area, it was planted with vines to satisfy the steadily increasing demand for wine

This page: Chateau Yaldara, near Lyndoch, is one of the most imposing wineries. The top photograph shows its fine facade, and the bottom photograph is of some of the antique furniture in its main hall. Despite its traditional appearance it was built quite recently, after Mr Hermann Thumm took over an old winery in 1947

This page: These wineries are among the largest in the Valley. The top photograph shows a picturesque corner of Yaldara winery, and in the centre is the famous clock tower of Yalumba. The massive cellars of Seppeltsfield, shown at foot of page, have been maturing good wine for the better part of a century

Facing page, top: A panoramic view from the Trial Hill Road lookout

Facing page, bottom: A characteristic Valley scene. This vineyard is one of the many which grow around Tanunda

Top Looking out over Rowland Flat towards Gramp's Orlando winery, and the hills beyond

Bottom Another Valley industry; the sand pits above Rowland Flat

Top: These great pot stills at Penfold's winery, Nuriootpa, are used to distil brandy. Fine brandy is distilled from the fermented juice of grapes which usually are grown specially for the purpose

Bottom: Straight from the vineyards, these grapes are on their way to becoming wine. These men at Kaiser-Stuhl (left) and at Chateau Tanunda (right) are tipping and loading them into the crushing hoppers

This page, top: The modern buildings of the Church of the Strait Gate, at Light Pass, stand next to the tower and spire of the original church

This page, centre: The lych gate stands in front of Collingrove chapel. Originally Baptist, now Church of England, the chapel was built by John Howard Angas in 1874 and belongs to the Angas estate

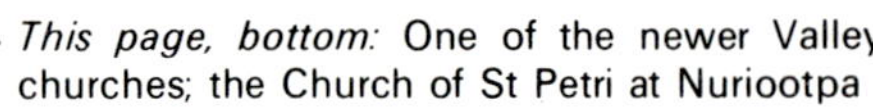

This page, bottom: One of the newer Valley churches; the Church of St Petri at Nuriootpa

Facing page, top: Coulthard House, Nuriootpa, was originally a home. Now it is a Folk Museum

Facing page, bottom left: The bold classic architecture of the Seppelt mausoleum always appeals to tourists

Facing page, bottom right: The tower and spire of Immanuel Church, Light Pass, rises above a neighbouring vineyard

Facing page, top: Low-temperature fermentation vats at Gramp's Orlando winery

Facing page, bottom: Storage vats in which Valley wines lie quietly maturing

Top left: When the grapes are ripe, most Valley people are busy in the vineyards

Centre: Summer scene in the North Para River, near Tanunda

Bottom: Barossa Valley pattern; rows of vines and rolling hills

This page: The biennial Vintage Festival is a great Valley occasion. Each township and most of the wineries prepare an elaborately decorated float to take part in the procession, and the feasting, sports, and dancing of the Vintage Fair are accompanied by plenty of good Valley wines. At top is the float from Marananga, and those at centre and bottom are from Kaiser Stuhl winery and Nuriootpa

Facing page, top: About fifteen hundred people attend the Weingarten Dinner during the Vintage Festival (*photo: Douglass Baglin*)

Facing page, bottom: The Maypole Dance makes a colourful spectacle at the Vintage Fair

Choosing a Vintage Queen is one of the great events at the Vintage Fair. At foot of page, contestants selected by the ten Valley towns arrive to take part in the Festival Grape-picking Championship. At right is Miss Helen Keightley, a recent Barossa Valley Vintage Queen *(photos by W. St. C. Johnson for S.A. Govt. Tourist Bureau)*

Top: Water supplies offered by the North and South Para Rivers, and numerous creeks, were among the attractions of the Valley for early settlers. This placid pool is in the North Para River as it circles Tanunda

Bottom: Barossa Valley folk are music-lovers. The Tanunda *Liedertafel* (song table) is a choral society founded in 1861, and the annual Tanunda Band Competitions, first held in 1910, attract competitors from numerous Valley towns and from other parts of Australia. The musicians below are those of the Tanunda Town Band, marching in a Vintage Festival procession (*photo: S.A. Govt. Tourist Bureau*)

Facing page: Valley scenes. At left is the church at Stockwell

This page: Some of the colourful signs which direct visitors to the Valley wineries

Facing page, bottom: Mares and foals of the Lindsay Park Stud being led out to pasture in a lucerne paddock

This page, top: Harvesting continues at Marananga while the setting sun casts long shadows

This page, left: Four more examples of Barossa winery signs

Facing page, top: The Barossa Motel, near Lyndoch, is one of those built to accommodate the increasing number of visitors. Guests in the dining-room may sip Barossa Valley wine as they look out over vineyards and hills

Facing page, bottom: Two Valley industries come together. The Angaston cement works as seen from some contour-planted Saltram vineyards

Top left: The Angaston Hotel was opened on Christmas Eve, 1846. Since then it has been rebuilt five times, but the building as it stands now is largely as it appeared in 1914

Top right: A visit to South Australia is incomplete without a tour of the Barossa Valley. Thousands of visitors, from many parts of the world, travel through the Valley each year

This page, bottom: The Nuriootpa Community Swimming Pool is an example of the amenities provided by community effort in the Valley townships

Top: "Where it all began." In 1847, Johann Gramp planted the first Valley vineyard at Jacob's Creek. This vineyard still grows there around the old cellars; part of the Gramp's Orlando winery. Gramp was closely followed by Joseph Gilbert, who founded the Pewsey Vale vineyard in 1847; by Samuel Smith in 1849; and by Joseph Seppelt in 1850

Right and bottom: Many of South Australia's seventy-three wineries and distilleries are situated in the Barossa Valley. The visitor can buy wine from those founded more than a century ago, or from those of a comparatively recent "vintage"

This page, top: The traditional craft of coopering is still carried on in Valley wineries. Harry Mahlo, cooper at Yalumba winery, heats barrel staves so that they can be bent into shape

This page, bottom: The Tolley, Scott and Tolley's distillery at Nuriootpa still uses the old wooden "coffee" stills for making brandy

Facing page, top: The modern automatic grape-crusher at Penfold's winery is a far cry from the wooden hand-presses originally used in the Valley

Facing page, bottom: The Old Bottling Store at Seppeltsfield gives visitors their choice of many fine wines

Pick the
right
sherry

This traditional harvest scene of stooks and stubble, near Ebenezer, is a reminder that the first settlers in the Valley devoted themselves to the same type of mixed farming which they had carried on in Germany. Despite the steadily growing importance of the grape, Valley farmers still grow good crops of grain